811.6   3874900   S0-CLY-871
JOH   Johnson, Sandra.
         My poetic expressions

KD

ROSE CREEK PUBLIC LIBRARY
4476 TOWNE LAKE PKWY.
WOODSTOCK, GA 30189

SEQUOYAH REGIONAL LIBRARY

3 8749 0061 4086 8

My Poetic Expressions

by

Sandra Johnson

authorHOUSE®

**PROPERTY OF
THE SEQUOYAH REGIONAL
LIBRARY SYSTEM CANTON, GA.**

AuthorHouse™
1663 Liberty Drive, Suite 200
Bloomington, IN 47403
www.authorhouse.com
Phone: 1-800-839-8640

© 2008 Sandra Johnson. All rights reserved.

*No part of this book may be reproduced, stored in a retrieval system, or
transmitted by any means without the written permission of the author.*

First published by AuthorHouse 1/9/2008

ISBN: 978-1-4343-4145-7 (sc)
ISBN: 978-1-4343-4144-0 (hc)

Printed in the United States of America
Bloomington, Indiana

This book is printed on acid-free paper.

Table of Contents

Introduction

Communication Writing 3

Spiritual

Let God 7
Awesome Power 8
My Search Has Ended 9
Grateful To Wake Up 10
A Talk With Jesus 11
The Greatest Gift 12
Keep Your Eyes On Jesus 13
Whenever I awake 14
Stand Still and Listen 15
Because You Asked Not 16
Hold On and Don't Let Go 17
Listen For Understanding 18

Love

A Thankful Beginning 21
Since You Came Into My Life 22
What I Feel For You 23
Without You...24
Special Vows 25
When I Think of You 26
Capture By Your Love 27
Forever With You 28
You Were the One 29
Our Perspective 30

Family

One Hundred Years 33
My Loving Mother..34
About Daddy..35

My Mother 36

Sadness

Moments Alone 39
When Night Falls 40
A Ride With "Good Times" 41
No More Sadness 42
Know Yourself 43
Wasted Time 44
Real Pain 45
Stop Lying 47
Heart Break 48
We Are Through 49
The Wet Wall 51

Abstract

Relaxation 55
Forgiveness 56
Future Hope 57
The Upper Hand 58
My Life's Puzzle 59
No Satisfaction 60
The Motionless Ball 61
A Temporary Stay 62
Beware 63
Journey of Life 64
Mind Your Own Business 65
Conquering Uncertainty 66
Be Careful What You Say 67
Creative Conversation 68
Just to Live 69
Easy Being Me 70
Evening Sunset 71
Facing Reality 72
Incarcerated 73
When I Get Out 74
Demolition 75

Mid-Night View 77
The Setting Sun 78
Let the Sky Be the Limit 79

Happiness

Inner Peace 83
Happiness 84
Spreading Happiness 85
Special Times..86
Happiness on High...87
Free Being Me...88
The Sojourn 89
Inspiring Words..90
It's Left Up To You..91

Introduction

Communication Writing

Words can communicate
the thoughts you have inside.
They express your emotions,
exposing you open and wide.

Sharing thoughts with others
who appreciate your view,
make it seem worthwhile
and very interesting too.

My admiration of words,
some seem to share the same.
I have been writing for a while
with the "play on words" game.

Communicating words,
in a way that is unique,
can be very profound
when you begin to speak.

Listeners lighten up
with a sparkle in their eye,
amazed at word combinations
which causes them to sigh.

So, conversations with paper
or writing for a release,
can be good therapy;
'Cause it lets your mind have peace!

Spiritual

Let God

Plans don't always work out
the way you want it to.
It makes you want to scream and shout,
not knowing what to do.

No matter what your age,
sometimes you want to quit.
Take it to the next stage,
then you can work with it.

You should know that crying
only fills you with doubt.
If you keep on trying,
eventually things'll work out.

Always pray and believe;
God will help in your decisions;
your desires you will achieve;
with Him you'll use precision.

The plan God has for you
may not match what you had in mind.
Just relax and let God through
'Cause His plans work every time!

Awesome Power

The power of your love
can grant my every wish.
Shining from up above,
anything I can accomplish.

With sun rays from the sky
to energize my soul.
It causes a spiritual high;
It's something I can't let go.

You refresh my thoughts with rain
that sprinkle gently on me.
You shower away my pain,
as I draw closer to Thee.

You send me enough wind
to scatter all of my fears.
My sorrows you attend
by wiping away my tears.

So when storms come my way,
You are there every hour.
I can never be dismayed
'Cause I have your awesome power!

My Search Has Ended

The plans I made for my life
never seem to come out right.
Something was always missing
and success was nowhere in sight.

So my wants were not fulfilled,
but daily my needs were met.
Still, there was something missing,
but I could not find it yet.

My rent was paid monthly,
so I'd have a place to stay.
I continued to search for something
and I searched for it everyday.

Health was never my problem;
Sickness didn't know where I lived.
That something was so hard to find,
Nobody knew what I would give.

But one day I finally realized...
What really was missing in my life.
It was <u>SOMEONE</u> and not <u>SOMETHING</u>
and His name is Jesus Christ.

At last my search has ended
and I'm not looking for anything,
'Cause Jesus is my Savior...
Yes, He is my everything.

Grateful To Wake Up

When I awake every morning,
I am thinking of you.
I watch the new day dawning
and the ground that's filled with dew.

The birds are starting to sing,
happy and cheery songs.
Throughout the neighborhood, it rings,
with everyone singing along.

Soon the sun is shining,
Brightening up the day.
It is your perfect timing
that awakes us everyday.

The blue sky is the background
with a few clouds sprinkled about.
The music is made of nature sounds
it is never turned up too loud.

Each day, I am blessed to wake up
'Cause you are thinking of me.
No way can it be called Luck
'Cause it was your will to be.

Thank you Dear Lord for Your love
that you continue to give.
All praises to You, above,
for as long as I shall live.

A Talk With Jesus

Yes, I had a talk with Jesus
when I could not go back to sleep.
If I kept my trust in Him,
He said He would forever keep.

He said that I could talk to Him,
whether it was day or night.
He already knew my problem;
He said that I would be alright.

I thanked Him for being with me
'Cause I had a very long day.
...thanked Him for our conversation;
I was so glad that He could stay.

So when I had fallen asleep,
however, I cannot recall.
I did not hear anymore noise,
just like having soundproof walls.

When I awoke the next morning,
I had a big smile on my face.
...Remembered my talk with Jesus
and how He brightened up my place.

Now, whenever I want to talk
Loudly, I call to my Jesus.
I know He's there for you and me;
No, He would never, ever leave us.

The Greatest Gift

Every good and perfect gift
comes from God, the Father.
He knows exactly what you need
each second, minute, and hour.

He gives us each a specialty
that's easy for us to do.
He lets it come so naturally;
It comes uniquely to you.

He loves us unconditionally,
with grace and mercy galore.
He'll give us the desires of our heart,
so praise Him more and more.

Your light will shine so brightly
in the darkest of the night.
It will be a contagious glow
that will soothe a doubtful sight.

The only good and perfect gift,
who cannot be forgotten,
is Jesus Christ, the greatest one
our Father's only begotten.

Keep Your Eyes On Jesus

Keep your eyes on Jesus
and always focus on Him.
He will guide and teach you
then "Sin" cannot enter in.

Keep your eyes on Jesus,
on the straight and narrow.
Through all the tribulations,
keep your eyes on the sparrow.

Keep your eyes on Jesus,
when friends don't treat you right.
Talk it over with Jesus,
any day or any time of the night.

Keep your eyes on Jesus,
whatever your trials may be.
With Him, your vision is perfect.
With Him, you can clearly see.

Keep your eyes on Jesus,
'Cause He is the main link.
Don't be like Peter on the water,
having doubt can make you sink.

So, keep your eyes on Jesus,
'Cause focus is a must.
He will catch you if you stumble,
but first, you have to trust.

Whenever I awake

Whenever I awake,
I know You brought me through.
A journey some never complete...
My thanks go straight to You.

Anything could have happened....
Maybe I could have been lost.
But with your Divine Guidance,
I'm blessed that You were my Boss.

All I had to do was to
totally depend on Your word.
It says You'll never forsake me
and that's not all I've heard.

I'm glad that You are with me,
every step of the way.
I know I could never make it;
Now, I'm thanking You without delay.

Therefore, whenever I awake,
it is because of Your love.
I'm glad that I am Your child
and it's me You're thinking of!

Stand Still and Listen

Each time you are obedient,
to the plans that God has for you.
Surely, He will pave the roads,
for you to go safely through

You do not have to worry
about what others have to say.
God knows what He is doing.
All you have to do is obey.

If you stand on God's word,
no way can you ever fall.
'Cause you are on a foundation
that cannot crumble at all.

Whatever God does for you,
will make others open their eyes,
to see the blessings bestowed,
After that, want Him in their lives.

Never do you want to miss
any message that God has today.
So just stand still and listen
to everything, He has to say!

Because You Asked Not

All the things that you say you want
but have not yet acquired.
Waiting on dreams to be fulfilled
without having a strong desire.

Always doing the same old thing,
by wishing with all your might.
Waiting, hoping, they will come true...
There is no vision in your sight.

The Master's there to lend an ear,
to answer your every call.
Never will He forsake his child
He'll always be there for us all.

Don't hesitate next time you need;
Just cry out and call His name.
He is there to rescue you
and never will He change.

So, be sincere when you pray,
then you'll receive your lot.
In the Bible it is written,
You have not because you asked not!

Hold On and Don't Let Go

The answers to all our questions
are always found inside
the real you, from God
can never ever hide

He knows well your destiny
before you can find your way
you are to keep on searching
'cause you'll find it one day

some decisions you made yesterday
in your heart, you knew wasn't right
haste could have played a vital factor
so you had a blurry sight

now everything seems clearer
and one more chance is needed
to plow the crop expected
and examine the grounds you seeded

so you ask, "What happens next?" . . .
I say, go to God in prayer
His plans will soon be revealed
and remember He'll always be there

The sooner you start to realize it,
peace will fill you throughout
I believe that wholeheartedly
and without a bit of doubt

Any problem you have to handle
certainly, I know God can
Thank Him for lighting your path
and don't let go of His hand!

Listen For Understanding

I pray for understanding
to get my life's full meaning.
So, on God's word I am standing;
It is God, who I am leaning.

No doubt, I trust Him completely
'Cause He's never failed me yet.
My Father loves me very deeply;
It is to Him, I owe my debts.

I know He listens to my call
that's why I try to do what's right.
It makes me want to do MY all,
Just to be acceptable in His sight.

Now, constantly, I am listening
for God to give my directions.
I try to hear Him whispering
because I WANT the connection.

So, if I am listening more
Understanding I will see.
All the plans God has in store,
I can apply individually.

Love

A Thankful Beginning

Pondering thoughts of yesterday,
I often think of you.
Because you knew just what to say,
to make happiness pursue.

All the times we've been together,
each one seemed anew.
I know our love will last forever
before our life is through.

I'm glad we had the chance to meet,
so many years ago.
My life would not be complete;
If you, I did not know.

So thank you for being a friend,
In my time of need.
Together we cannot help but win.
Now others can follow our lead.

Since You Came Into My Life

Whenever you're on my mind,
I want you here with me.
I think of you all the time,
In dreams and reality.

Anxiety gets my best
until our meeting again.
I cannot settle for less;
You are my fortune and fame.

I trust you know my heart
and how it beats for you.
I felt this from the start,
piercing me all the way through.

Every breath that I take,
is how I long for you.
My love is not a mistake,
eternally it will endure.

So happy, I have become
since we have been together.
Certainly, you are the one
with whom I will live forever.

What I Feel For You

I am truly glad I met you
it's been more than a year ago
I am hoping you feel as I do
because inside my heart, I know

sure you are very intelligent
but you already know this is true
with all of your grace and elegance
only adds to the "why" I love you

just because you have graduated
from your hometown school
does not mean you are situated
to face life with only its rules

however, what's in store for you
will be on a much higher level
compared to what you've been use to
it will be like that forever

life is so unpredictable
and no day exactly the same
just make yourself more flexible
then the longer you'll be in the "game"

life will be very challenging
but you will handle it well
be cautiously analyzing
surely, you will feel compelled

so, whatever your goals may be
I, really wish success to you
but clearly, I want you to see
that always, I'll be there for you!

Without You

I cannot live without you
'Cause I want you by my side.
It's one of the things that you can do,
to help me to survive.

You walking through life with me,
will be like an evening stroll...
Us holding hands so lovingly...
Together, we'll never grow old.

Just enjoying our company,
on the road to happiness.
Realizing that the bumps to be,
will not be more, but less.

You and I can be as one,
as long as we, both agree
...That we must have lots of fun
while building our unity.

I cannot live without you,
if we cannot linger in love.
I know we can make it through
'Cause we have guidance from above.

Special Vows

Because our vows were special,
it seems like yesterday.
Each said with conviction,
to last forever and a day.

Never we wanted to part,
so marriage made us as one.
Blessings were showered by God;
It was His will be done.

When I start to ponder,
on how our union began.
I have to smile and think...
How fortunate I truly am.

'Cause life with you has been
better than most would expect.
It is so close to perfect,
to me, it's the best thing yet.

All of this time together
is what was meant to be.
The years have passed so quickly;
It's part of our destiny.

Because our vows were special,
I know you feel as I do.
I am so appreciative
because you love me too!

When I Think of You

Before you came along,
my life was filled with doubt.
So now that I have you,
I'll never be without.

You have made a difference,
to make my life complete.
So what would of happened? . . .
If you, I did not meet.

I want to tell the world
how very special you are.
Surely you have become
my personal earthly star.

You have made me happy;
I smile thinking of you.
I'm so truly blessed
to have my dream come true.

So thank you, for letting me
be who I really am.
'cause I really thank God
for sending you, My Man!

Capture By Your Love

So many years ago,
you totally captured my heart.
Locked in by Cupid's door,
I welcomed it from the start.

Sedated by your affection,
daily my cravings build.
Our unity is a reflection,
an example of God's will.

Never will I regret
being isolated by your love.
I am grateful that we met
and graced by God above.

May our journey be rich
with life's little treasures.
...with everlasting love which
can never be measured.

In my heart you will stay,
for as long as I shall live.
For your love, I 'd gladly pay,
but my heart, I freely give.

Forever With You

Being with you forever
will not be enough for me.
Fate has put us together
fulfilling our destiny.

Every moment we share
fills my heart with joy.
Just knowing that you are there;
It is you, I truly adore.

You are the beam of light,
brightening my "nighted" path.
Us being together is right;
each time we do the math.

So, whatever we now share,
encompassing nurturing years.
I know you're fully aware
that I'll always want you near.

Forever will not be long,
if only I can spend it with you.
No, my love cannot be wrong,
especially, if you feel like I do!

You Were the One

When I was starting out,
you were there for me.
I'm glad you had no doubt;
You gave me security.

Really, you do not know
how you impacted my life.
Truly, you helped me to grow;
You put my service in the light.

These words cannot fully express
all that I want to say.
However, you were the best.
Therefore, this I must convey.

Never will I forget
the relationship we have shared.
Surely, I have no regrets
'cause I know how much you cared.

Honestly, you were the one
who became my guiding star.
Thank you for all you have done,
in helping me to get this far!

Our Perspective

What I see
while looking at you
is a part of me
from a different view.

The stare in your eye
reflects back to mine,
not knowing why
it's that way by design.

Sometimes you say
the words in my thought.
My answers display;
Our concepts caught.

What we share
is possessed by one.
... is somewhat rare
but it's not uncommon.

This basic description
is what I perceive.
It is what I've given
And totally believe.

I hope your view
while looking at me
is a part of you
PERSPECTIVELY!

Family

One Hundred Years

One hundred years is a long time
to live as a human being.
You have managed to do just that
because you were born with good genes.

Certainly, what you have been through
is amazing beyond compare.
.. .'cause not everyone will make it
to the road that can take them there.

Over the years I have witnessed
how prayerful and honest you've been.
How you truly trusted in God,
I know that Jesus was your friend.

There's no way could you have made it
without the beliefs you possessed.
God has always been there for you.
...and you, He has totally blessed

As you reflect back on your life,
may the regrets you had, be few.
I hope that you will be more happy
when you hear me say, "I love you!"

My Loving Mother

Because you're you,
loving you is easy.
Like breathing fresh air,
I feel good knowing that
our love is mutual.

My confidant.
My friend.
My one and only Mother,
You have held my hand
since birth.

You have watched adulthood
invade my naive ways.

Through nonsense,
you found a way to insert logic.

Through awkwardness,
you helped me to walk
the straight and narrow.

Throughout my entire life,
you were the dominant influence.

Now Mother,
I want to express my gratitude,
with abundance!

About Daddy

Sometimes when I stop and think back
on all the years that has gone by,
with amazing things accomplished
It is something I cannot deny.

My view of life was in color.
Some days filled with reds and yellows,
others with new green and sad blue,
but, my view was mostly mellow.

The more I think of you these days
with the eyes of maturity.
I realize you gave me love,
as well as my security.

I am glad that you are my Dad;
This is a part of your knowing.
With love for you, my heart is filled
and sometimes overflowing.

So thank you, Dad for everything,
for all your care and concern.
As one of my teachers of life,
there is a lot from you I've learned!

My Mother

The special woman in my life
happened to be my mother.
To my father, she was a wife
that's why I wanted no other.

I knew my mother loved me
with her entire heart.
I knew this as a baby;
I felt it from the start.

During the early years,
my mother guided my path.
She wiped away my naive tears
when I could not do my math.

Whenever I felt the need,
just to talk about whatever,
my mother had time for me
through sunny or stormy weather.

My mother took good care of
all of her children and spouse.
Continuously her surplus of love
permeated our house.

The qualities she possessed
was amazing beyond compare.
With her I was truly blessed
just to have her there.

God knew what He had done
when He gave my mother to me.
He knew she was the one
who would love me, for me!

Sadness

Moments Alone

There is a calm
that hovers in the air.

Dreams are now in play,
Deep thoughts in focus.

This time alone
will soon be flown,
and I must arise to meet
the rising sun,
which brings in its glow
appointed times and scheduled routines
(Some enjoyed,
others dreaded).

But eventually,
the calm,
the stillness will again come,
a part of Earth's cycle,
forever to be.

When Night Falls

WHEN NIGHT FALLS,

so does emptiness and loneliness.
Like rain from heaven
in the sunny noonday,
the pitch of darkness
manifests itself
from the depths of the soul.
The vacancy crescendos
with every second that quickly passes by.
Eventually, the unbearable hurt
must be unpressurized.
Suddenly,
the embankment cracks
and the water trickles
then with a steady stream.
Relief comes with the wall collapsing.
Finally, rest comes with reluctant sleep.
However, realizing tomorrow is another day
filled with scheduled routines, but

WHEN NIGHT FALLS!

A Ride With "Good Times"

I won't remember the hurt of yesterday

'cause the pain goes deep within.

My "Good Times" went for a ride out of town,

then, got lost.

So I'm waiting and hoping for its return

'cause I need more than a <u>few</u> "Good Times"

to feel complete.

No, I won't remember yesterday,

but ponder tomorrow,

when I can ride around town,

in "Good Times" car!

No More Sadness

Feeling sad sometimes
makes me wonder why.
What happened to the sunshine
that's missing in the sky.

The color of my sadness
is a dark and grayish blue.
It fills the room with madness
that it portrays a gloomy hue.

Sadness, I already told
that it has to go away
'cause I'm getting too old
to be filled with such dismay.

It's time for joy and happiness
to spend some time with me.
It's going to be my business
to fill my life with glee.

So no more sadness for me
and even the sun will shine.
Now I'm waiting eagerly;
Happiness, it's our time!

Know Yourself

Things are not what they seem
when, at first, you take a look.
It is your judgmental gleam
that says you know the book.

You cannot turn the cover
when you take a glance.
You cannot even hover
all pages, you have to prance.

Once through the entire book
will not make you well versed.
There will be things overlooked
many things not seen at first.

Surprised is what you would be,
to see how others saw you.
You would think more cautiously
with whatever came into your view.

So don't pretend to know everything
only about everybody else.
...'cause you cannot know anything
until you get to know yourself.

Wasted Time

Tear drops on my pillow
'cause I've been crying over you.
You keep on doing the very thing
that you should never do.

Frustration keeps on building
so high I cannot see through.
Just learn to keep your promises
and do what you said you'd do.

All this crying that I've done
is leaving my eyes so red.
I know that I'm not dreaming
and it's not just in my head.

I know you will not change
because of the time that has passed.
Things could be so much better,
but my life is going by fast.

Love is what keeps me here
but it is too blind to see.
...that I cannot be myself
when I cannot even be happy.

I'd rather have tears of joy,
to freely flow from my eyes.
I would be laughing so hard
I'd be glad I was alive.

So no more crying over you;
I guess you're just being yourself.
From now on, it's all about me.
And I'm "gonna" be myself.

Real Pain

How can I explain
the pain I feel inside.
My life is not the same;
It's something I can't hide.

The hurt is deep within
which causes tears to flow.
But only time can mend
my broken heart, though.

Comprehension is gone,
leaving confusion behind.
Even reasons have flown
without a telltale sign.

It seems that when I dwell
on this unwanted ache,
then my heart starts to swell...
How much am I to take?

Havoc is what I've reeked
to prevent a gnawing through.
But my heart is now weak
'cause it has split into two.

The echoes of this suffering
shout throughout my soul.
Strength is what I'm mustering
to survive until I am old.

Patience is what I need
to ride out this storm.
Then my heart will not bleed,
nor will I have to mourn.

Real Pain *continued*

No way will you ever know,
how I really feel.
Unless you've been there before,
you can't know pain for real!

Stop Lying

You keep on lying to me
'cause you cannot tell the truth.
You say that you have changed,
but with "Lying", you have a truce.

You say what you're going to do;
I listen and you sound so real.
However, I keep on forgetting that
with the devil, you've made a deal.

Every time I catch you lying,
I don't want to associate with you.
But then say to myself,
"What would my Jesus do?"

I feel that you're dating Satan
and with "Lying", you have a romance.
I deeply feel that my Jesus
would give you another chance.

So for now, I'll keep on praying
that you will stop your lies.
I'll pray that you'll seek God
and with Satan, you will cut all ties.

...because then and only then
will you want to tell the truth...
'cause when you give up your lying,
Satan will have to turn you loose!

Heart Break

Fluttering fast

    out of control

        surprisingly injured

           by unbearable suffering

        Beating with confusion

    while wondering why

constantly echoing

    a replay of pain

        Since sniper shots

           targeted my heart

           the invasion of fear

has caused me to

        Rapidly, Rampantly, Run

           . . . Looking for cover!

We Are Through

Why did you even tell me
that I was the one for you?
Now I have found out
that you did not tell the truth.

Why did you have to lie?
You could have been "up front".
You did not have to lead me on
for all of these months.

I was open and honest
with everything I said.
Now I am trying to understand,
why you're "messing"with my head?

So, why did you deceive me
from the very first start?
I thought you were sincere
and not play games with my heart.

I am slightly confused
about your reasons why.
Now, I am stunned and numbed;
I cannot even to cry.

You know what you did to me
will come back to you multiplied.
'cause what you did to me
goes deeper than your lies.

So now the time has come
for me to move along.
I'm not going to sit and mope;
my feelings for you are gone.

We Are Through *continued*

I know I deserve the best
and I thought that it was you.
But since you proved me wrong,
our relationship is through!

The Wet Wall

Crawling so swiftly
  the wave of the water
    over ran the panicking people.
      Climbing a plus thirty feet,
        conquering everything and everybody,
          smothering the helpless cries,
            filling the human cavities
            like an overflowing glass of water.
            Forcing the last breath of life
          into the sea.
          Whipping and splashing with a mighty roar,
        thousands of unsuspecting individuals
        who were waiting on tomorrow.
      Now, who are here no more.
      waves that had no competition,
        with one swoop, easily won the war.
        All the time,
      thinking she was entitled to rise and fall at will,
      destroying villages, land, trees, animals, and people.
      This wet wall was not listening
      to the pleas of mercy or reason,
    just intent on
    making the weak and strong
    stumble and fall,
never independently vertical, again
...softly and powerfully
    causing a humbling and
      a calling to the omniscient and to the omnipotent
      for deliverance.

      Truly, this was a day of Baptism
        by the giant waves, some call Tidal,
          but what we call Tsunami!

Abstract

Relaxation

Cool, breezy,

taking it easy.

What's happening?

Important?... not in the least

Why? ...

Floating requires no effort

Rest, let it be

moment aft moment,

feeling better and better

should not life be equal?

Never worrying, Never wondering.

Just letting whatever comes . . . WELCOME!

Forgiveness

there is a place in your heart
that is as big as it can be.
I knew right from the start
that forgiveness was there for me.

I'm sorry for all the things
I might have said or done.
I am sorry for everything,
so please don't ever run.

Sincerely, I'm asking you
to let by-gones be gone.
'Cause if you thought it through
you'll know I'm not alone.

Mistakes have been made
by some of the best people. I know.
Don't let our friendship fade
'cause separate ways, we'll go.

Forgiveness know s you well,
now you can introduce him to me.
From the beginning, I could tell
that our relationship should be!

Future Hope

My understanding of tomorrow

is that of hope.

'cause when feelings are optimistic,

anything can happen.

I believe only goodness will be my friend

and my mercy follow me through my life.

Yes, I can now breathe with relief ...

I've got my second wind

and now I know my trip to the future,

however short or long,

can be made with confidence!

The Upper Hand

All my life,

I have experienced the Yo-Yo SYNDROME,

up and down,

up and down,

But frequently, my life would get stuck.

It seemed that mostly I was down,

'cause sometimes the glue that held my life together,

completely dried up.

. . .Then life for me just fell apart . . .

But I hung on

because I knew that with one shake of the wrist,

I would be up again.

Once up,

I decided I needed more control over my life

so I took the upper hand,

'cause what goes <u>down</u> must come <u>up</u>.

Now, my ups and downs are equal!

My Life's Puzzle

My thoughts of the future
lingered throughout today.

My wanting more good things and
knowing I can get it,
leaves out the specifics,
especially "How?"

My future is just like a million piece puzzle
with at least half the pieces missing . . .

It seem impossible to put my life together.
So, now two questions come to my mind:

Should I play another game of life?

Or

Should I look for the missing pieces?

No Satisfaction

Satisfaction seems to elude me
it peeks and runs away.
As soon as it sees me,
I think it wants to stay.

Then I am left unfulfilled
just like the times before.
Up, I don't want to give;
My lack makes me want it more.

How long can I do without?
My feeling are overflowing.
I'm so furious I want to shout.
With yearning, my heart's over pouring

Satisfaction is very nice,
somewhere I read it to be so.
Will suffering by my price?
...Truly pain will make it cost more.

I think I'll invite satisfaction
to come over for some tea.
If thirst have to be the attraction,
I know it will quench it for me!

The Motionless Ball

My world is round . . .

like a ball that bounces.

When it goes up, I am happy.

When it goes down, I am sad.

Right now,

the ball is half-way between up and down.

The problem is . . .

I don't know if

the ball is on its way up

or on its way down.

But I do know ...

I feel suspended in mid-air.

So, should I be prepared to fall
or

should I ^{jump} for joy!

A Temporary Stay

The bondage of the soul causes

wonderment of the world outside

the surrounding bars manifested limitations

which only let the same view be focused

in addition , pacing back and for the on the floor

of the cornered mind, time is unknown

just think only of the guard who bears the key

to the door of freedom, and then hope can be built

finally when captivity is over

this painful confinement will be remembered

as one of life's unfortunate experiences.

Beware

Living life can be strange ...

'cause every situation is like someone

who do not know.

With the same token, (every now and then)

one does meet a situation that is familiar.

Therefore, confidence can be experienced . . .

'cause the unknown is nowhere in sight.

Yes, no fears

no worries,

no need for apparent concern.

But remember, when life becomes strange,

live cautiously and carry a little mace!

Journey of Life

Walking the streets of life
is like walking through the jungle
walk softly with a big knife
speaking in a whisper or a mumble

armed with some protection
you will always be ready
no matter what your direction
just keep your pace steady

your path will not be clear
when nighttime gradually comes
your good instincts must be near
so you'll know when to walk or run

the journey that you will take
will test your entire soul
it's a trip we will have to make
though we'll never be in control!

Mind Your Own Business

If you would mind you business
and leave all of ours alone,
you would have more time
to mind just your own.

Your business would be successful
and we would be happy too...
'cause our business will be ours
and not left up to you

but that will never happen,
it'll be too good to be true.
You cannot leave us alone;
you'd be lost with nothing to do.

What do you think we did
before you tried to take charge?
We knew how to handle our business
that's why we handled ours.

With all the meddling you do,
we will never ever condone.
Just learn to mind your business
and please, leave ours alone!

Conquering Uncertainty

Where are you going now?
Do you even know the way?
Is the road to your future
Lit with the sun today?

You, too, have many questions
That you could certainly ask . . .
But you are not the only one
who has been given such a task.

Wisdom comes with age.
And to some it's not given.
Some of us can't comprehend
'cause we are too busy living.

Life is filled with uncertainties
just to make us think . . .
about how we can stay afloat
when it is so easy to sink.

Constant fear of the unknown
is not what we should feel.
Continuing our confident search
should be our main appeal.

No matter what road you're on
step with blessed assurance
until you reach your destiny
you'll need lots of endurance.

Be Careful What You Say

Why did you say the things you said?
Without my response to hear.
Others, now, have been misled;
My good name, you have smeared.

Thoughtfulness , you did not know
when my concerns were involved.
Never have I felt so low;
for sure, this must be resolved.

I thought that you were my friend,
but friends do not do what you did.
No helping hand would you lend.
So, from my feelings and me, you hid.

Your "SELF" spoke loudly to you...
"Nobody care about me!"
Your inner voice tells what you know
...'cause the real you cannot see!

My actions to you, will demonstrate
what friendship truly means.
...'cause an understanding relationship
can manifest more than it seems.

You need to treat your friends
with same respect that you deserve.
You should practice, again and again
then you won't step on their nerves.

Be careful next time, whatever you say,
especially if it's said in haste.
Having a dependable friend theses days
is a terrible thing to waste!

Creative Conversation

There is a title or label
when having good conversation
So it is nice to be able
to stimulate your sensations

Each moment with a unique style
statements lead into another
they go on for a while
all different from others

you are being spontaneous
and depending on what is said
spoken homogeneously
as if organized and then read

when bringing out a new design
creativity plays a role
with whatever the length of time
digging deep down into the soul

now you are set for retention
by learning something that is new
'cause you have focused attention
you have a optimistic view

Just to Live

I'm fortunate to be
                              to see
                              to feel life.

Reach out and touch my mind
                              my heart
                              my very soul.

... 'cause everyday I experience
                              a power surge that

constantly revs within . . .

and this electricity causes
                              an eagerness

to live my life with . . .

GRATITUDE!

Easy Being Me

The feeling flows

smoothly about me.

Making rounds ever so gently . . .

'causing easy thoughts

to become

reality.

Relaxing, enjoying, and being

"La Natural".

Feeling light and delicate,

living the moment to the "Max".

Just being carefree,

'cause being me

is all I can be!

Evening Sunset

As the evening tides
begin to soar
cool waves rush in
running to shore

A gentle breeze
caresses the air
with reminiscence
of times to spare

Observance of the ocean,
manifests mystery
like the heated sun
hot and blistery

Pendulum waves
with a hypnotic beat,
like synchronized dancers
taking a leap

A treasured encounter,
at euphoria's desk,
always in my memory,
will this evening be etched!

Facing Reality

Reality hits with power blows
blows hard enough to knock down
even the strongest

Facing him can sometimes
be as intimidating as
encountering the Boogy Man in the dark

Reality can come up behind you,
tap you on the shoulder
and as soon as you turn to see
who it is,
he says, "Boo"

With surprise written on your face,
you "strike up" a conversation
with "Mr. Big"

Before you finish, Reality gets you
to confess everything you knew all along

So, don't run away from Reality,
learn to face him
toe to toe

Then you won't be down
for the count!

Incarcerated

locked up to the city
the inmate cannot see
the freedom he used to have
that was not as costly

but behind the brick walls
are the cells that lock at night
are checked at every hour
to make sure that they are tight

viewing all the same faces
who share similar thoughts
who sometimes get frustrated
as well as over wrought

some who's been there many times
don't know what it's all about
just pretending to themselves
that soon they will get out

yes, just locked up to the city
without a key to his cell
he's a veteran to incarceration
with a sad story to tell

When I Get Out

As I sit here thinking,
thoughts bombard my mind.
Rapidly, my eyes start blinking. . .
Just calculating my time.

Thinking of what I would do
If I were out and about.
Goals that I would pursue
right now, I do not have any doubt.

But now I can only dream
of how I wish things were.
Nothing is what it seems,
reality is just a blur.

I trust my cal-cu-la-tions
are quick and precise for me.
I do not want complications
delaying where I could be.

Yes, one day at a time
is what I must surely take.
...while always keeping in mind
that this was just a mistake.

So, when I'm finally released
I will know what to do.
I will attain another lease
to start my life anew!

Demolition

In the early morning,
in the first few hours,
an airplane crashed
into the World Trade Tower.

Instantly killing men
and women while working,
there were few survivors
and death was for certain.

Only minutes later,
hit by another plane,
the second twin tower
also burst into flames.

Diligent rescue workers
were quick on the scene.
Nothing before imagined
could they have foreseen.

Assistance of all kinds
helped those who were hurt.
Doing whatever they could
...just trying to stay alert

when all of a sudden,
both towers started to crumble.
Tons of falling debris
caused the earth to rumble.

Panicking people were
running for their lives.
Many men and women
who were husbands and wives.

Why was this happening?
...it seemed like a dream...
Who could have done this?
And why were they so mean?

Now, the hunt is on
for those who are to blame.
Harborers of the enemy
will be punished the same.

The tall twin towers were
demolished before its time.
It left an enormous void
in our subconscious mind.

So, in the back of our throats
is a taste that is sour
whenever we think or speak of
the World Trade Towers.

Mid-Night View

Looking out of my window
during the mid night hour.
I see nocturnal beauty,
an overwhelming power.

The twinkling of the stars,
sparkling throughout the sky,
adorned with decorations,
pleasing to anyone's eye.

In attendance is the moon,
with all its alluring glow,
directly casting a light
on the objects found below.

Wallpaper of the heavens
painted only during night,
surely found the world over. . .
yes, a soothing peaceful sight.

Subsequently awaiting
for what the night has in store,
this exceptional moment
transporting pleasures galore.

The Setting Sun

As the sunset descended
daylight followed in turn.
Wind movement diminished,
a vivid peace I learned.

As the waves crawled to shore
for a brief moment in time,
it soon reversed direction,
a constant replay in my mind.

While this was happening,
a calm was realized,
joy and happiness appeared
directly in front of my eyes.

The scene was so beautiful,
doubts of reality flashed.
Orange shadows from the sunset
reflected the ocean's mass.

Soon the eye of the sun
closed itself to the day.
The warmth and rays it brought
had finally gone away.

Maybe tomorrow will promise
more or less of the same.
Maybe it will be different...
and just begin to rain!

Let the Sky Be the Limit

All of the limitations
that you put upon yourself,
build a wall of isolation,
dividing you and success.

Anything you desire
is something you can get.
But, the only thing required
is persistence and sweat.

With God as your guide,
you'll have no restrictions.
But, only you can decide
about your true convictions.

So, don't "box" yourself in
with no way to get out.
Anything is possible, when
you're not filled with doubt.

Just let yourself be free
and do not be so timid.
'cause when you focus, you will see
that the sky is the limit.

Happiness

Inner Peace

When I am happy,

I hear music

I hear laughter everywhere.

. . . That serene togetherness

of my soul,

is loudly content.

I then feel like dancing

to the rhythm in my heart,

and nothing at all seems to matter.

Thus, I can never tire

or the movement of my feet;

for every step is as though

I just began.

Happiness

Happiness is here to stay
inside my soul with me.
While sadness has gone away
on the ship sailing the sea.

I've been searching a long time
for happiness to find my place.
Now that happiness is all mine
even seconds I cannot waste.

Don't you want to find happiness
and everyday you can be glad?
Your inner happiness will be obvious.
Yes, seldom you will be sad.

So keep on looking for peace
to be happy just like me.
Then others will want your lease
'cause happiness is what they'll see!

Spreading Happiness

Happiness fills my heart with rhythmic cheer.

Now my soul can sing many happy tunes.

I am filled with much eagerness and gladness,

just to know that my spiritual cup doth runneth over.

Each morning when I rise, happiness seems to pierce my

entire existence and words cannot describe my gratification.

My happiness seems to remove obstacles and

replace them with a neatly paved path.

I'm glad happiness found my nighted days

and gave sunlight to my solid black nights.

Maybe my happiness will speak loudly so all can hear

. . . I hope my happiness is contagious!

Special Times

Smooth thoughts float

high on clouds of happiness

now the mellowness of the moment

soothes the soul

worries seem to melt

and dry on the concrete of freedom.

Thus, visions of surrounding beauty

are vividly manifested.

This utopic life atmosphere is

unfortunately temporary

however, this calmness and uniqueness will

not be forgotten . . . only recalled

time and time again!

Happiness on High

The clouds in my life

are used for transportation

to relaxation . . . so,

I jump on
and float
to and fro

even my reactions be come spontaneous

yes, I feel good being me

natural and uninhibited

with no stress . . . no strife

so, sporadically,
I elevate to the

"HIGH"
I feel inside!

Free Being Me

I try to do
the best I can
but people I know
don't understand

why I do
the things I do
it's the drummer's beat
I'm listening to

he sends messages
only I can hear
but to others
my response seem weird

I have to do
what seems right for me
I can't let anyone tell me
who I should be

my individuality
is what makes me ... me!

I fly high; I am glad I'm free.

The Sojourn

Cruising for happiness
before the sun sets
feelings of emptiness
but having no regrets

Sailing the vast sea
no matter what comes up
searching endlessly
for lasting comforts

Thinking of which directions
east, west, north or south
'cause "easy" is a misconception
choose when there is no doubt

the undulating waters
swaying the big boat
just following my orders
while trying to stay afloat

the sun sets beautifully
better than a painted picture
advancing religiously
like the Bible scriptures

knowing my destination
is just around the bend
starting positive sensations
for new beginnings, not the end

Inspiring Words

Words that are sprinkled on pages
display arrays of careful thought
it's been done throughout the ages
it's how some of us have be taught

the formation of all the words
can inspire or motivate
reminding you of something heard
that brought up a need for debate

inspiring words make you think
it gives your life a new meaning
it makes you think you found a link
to the purpose of your being

because of your inspiration
you can finally smile again
now you have the motivation
to the world your talents transcend

arrange your words the way you want
be sure to say what's on your mind
finding true perfection, you won't
it cannot happen every time

sprinkle your words creatively
so that others will want to read
COM-binate them positively
they'll think it's something they need

It's Left Up To You

Being motivated
is really left up to you.
No matter whatever happens,
it depends on what you do.

If you decide to sit
and wait at home alone,
do not expect a change
with the lack of interest shown.

You have to start to think
about your future goals.
... about how you can attain them
before you think, you're too old.

Because life will go on
for you and everybody else.
Don't you think you deserve more?
You should want to help yourself!

Whatever goals you want to reach,
eventually, you can acquire.
You have to really want it;
you have to have a desire.

So, stop your procrastination
and do what needs to be done.
Plan some steps of strategy,
then do them one by one.

So being motivated
is really left up to you.
Whatever your goals may be,
it depends on what you do!

About the Author

Sandra Grant Johnson was born in Brunswick, Georgia. Among her siblings, she is the third oldest of seven children and the oldest of four girls. She attended Risley Elementary School, Burroughs-Mollette Junior High, and Glynn Academy High School.

She received an Associate of Science Degree in Data Processing from Brunswick Junior College, now called Coastal Georgia Community College. After high school, Sandra married and had two sons, Derrick and Sean, whom she loves dearly. In 1998, she published a chapbook entitled "Planting a Good Seed...selected spiritual poems." In pursuit of higher education, Sandra enrolled at DeVry University in Decatur, Georgia to obtain a Bachelor's degree in Computer Engineering.

Printed in the United States
102272LV00004B/1-48/A